Joy Comes in the Morning: Lessons Learned Through Cancer

Jane Runkle

Joy Comes in the Morning:
Lessons Learned Through Cancer
by Jane Runkle

Cover photo by Sarah Runkle

ISBN: 1515140032
ISBN-13: 978-1515140030

DEDICATION

This book is dedicated to those who have shown me how to trust the Lord but the examples of their own lives, as they, too, have walked through suffering. First are Clarence and Elva Jane Perkins, my maternal grandparents, faithful believers and prayer warriors, who passed on a legacy of faith to my siblings and me. Second, I want to dedicate it to my own parents, Kathryn and Jerrald Daugherty, who were an example to all of us as they walked through suffering graciously by God's grace. Finally, I dedicate it to my husband, Dan Runkle, who is walking through life with me. I will always be grateful for his love for me and for our Lord.

CONTENTS

ACKNOWLEDGMENTS

I wish to thank those who helped us through this journey: my husband's parents, Terry and Beverly Runkle: my mother, Kathryn Daugherty; our siblings, Laura McConkey, Dan Daugherty and Chris Runkle, and their families: Joy Godby, who greatly helped us in Houston, Terry Daugherty and Amy Mollberg, my cousins who showed me kind hospitality, my friend and prayer warrior, Jean Seres, Lynwood Baptist Church in Cape Girardeau, MO; Southcliff Baptist Church in Fort Worth, TX, and my physicians, Dr. Booser, Dr. Strom, Dr. Ross, and Dr. Lyss. I am so grateful for all of their help and support as we went through our very difficult year. The Lord was so gracious to give us such family and friends.

I also want to thank Kathryn Daugherty, Daniel Runkle, Michal Watson, Sarah Runkle, and Grace Runkle for their helpful comments on the manuscript for this book.

.

INTRODUCTION

I'd like to take the distinct privilege of introducing you to my extraordinary wife, Jane. She is truly the excellent wife of Proverbs 31, and the crown described in Proverbs 12. She is the fruitful vine in my house described in Psalm 128, through whom the Lord has given me children like olive plants around my table. Yet every story has a beginning, so in my introduction of her, let me rewind the clock back to 1984 when the Lord was doing a transforming work in my life under the preaching of Dr. Charles Stanly in Atlanta, GA.

Back in 1984, I was sitting in my car there in the parking lot of Georgia Institute of Technology discussing with a dear brother in Christ our picture of the ideal woman, and how first meeting that woman might look. The Lord had put my friend, Steve Fulton, in my life for the purpose of discipleship. He was that person whom God used to bring me accountability, connect me with a small group fellowship of believers there at Tech, and help me repent from the "get out of Hell free ticket," counterfeit gospel, under which worldly lifestyle I had been living in slavery.

During that conversation in my 1984 Pontiac Fiero, Steve described meeting that person for the first time, but then immediately getting into an argument with her. Later, he figured, he and this woman would gain respect for one another and then grow madly in

1

love with one another. He might have said something to the effect of "you know, like a Spencer Tracey - Katherine Hepburn love story." I don't recall how much I let on to him about my take on his perfect scenario, but I remember thinking to myself, "That's the most absurd thing I've ever heard. Why would you want to start a lifelong loving relationship with an argument?" Little did Steve or I know that, within a year of that conversation, I would be meeting my future bride-to-be in the fashion he had described. It's funny to look back now on how Jane and I met, when I consider how harmonious our marriage has been.

In this short book, my wife shares her life and our journey "through the valley" in her battle, our family's battle, with fourth stage breast cancer. As you read, I think you will discover the truly extraordinary message of love that our Lord and Savior Jesus Christ has given us, and the truly extraordinary life that a believer who is yielded to Him can live.

Daniel Brett Runkle

1 BACKGROUND AND DIAGNOSIS

I was born in 1963 in Park Ridge, Illinois. My life started with a struggle, as I wasn't breathing when I was born. Mom had fibroid tumors that crowded me, and to say my birth was difficult would be an understatement. I was in such distress before my birth that there was not time to do a C-section. My mother's obstetrician, Dr. Dye, had to reach in and pull me out. When he and the rest of his team saw that I wasn't breathing, some in the room said, "Well, she'll just be a vegetable anyway." However, Dr. Dye would not give up and kept trying to resuscitate me. I finally began to breathe on my own but had seizures. I was kept in an isolette and given Phenobarbital to control the seizures.

My mom had been a high school English teacher, but stayed home to raise her children for many years after I was born. My dad was a high school chemistry teacher, but he was also an assistant football coach at his school. My mom liked to go to the football games there, and, since Dr. Dye lived nearby, my mom would drop me off at his house so he could babysit me and observe me, while she went to the games. At one point, knowing that education was very important to my parents, he told her, "I think I can promise you a C student." My mother, teacher that she was, found every possible way to stimulate my brain, and I did better in school than anyone would have thought when I was born. The Lord was gracious and not only saved me from death, but gave me miraculously good health besides.

I had a happy childhood. Our house was a two-story colonial on a quiet street in Palatine, a suburb of Chicago. My sister, Laura, was born a little less than two years after me, and my brother, Dan, was born in 1970. Since there were more than 30 school-age children on our block, we always found things to do. We played two-square with a ball, jumped rope, enjoyed Mankala, which we called "the marble game," and, perhaps best of all, we played "neighborhood." "Neighborhood" was an elaborate game, in which various porches and patios were places of business, garages were homes, and chalk was used to make parking spaces for our bicycles in the driveways. Our family's front porch was usually the hospital, and I was the physician. One neighbor's back porch was the beauty shop and one garage was turned into a school. We had to use our imaginations! We also loved to make snow forts in the winter, which included cubbyholes to store snacks.

Since both of my parents were teachers, education was, of course, very important in our family. I did well in school, but I struggled with perfectionism as a child and into adulthood. I had very high expectations for myself, which sometimes made me quite miserable. However, I loved learning and felt most contented working on math or reading a good book.

I was raised in the United Methodist Church, and I learned to love God and began to study His Word at an early age. I took our eighth grade confirmation class very seriously and, at that time, I asked Jesus to be Lord of my life. My relationship with the Lord was on again off again through high school and college, as there were areas of sin that interfered with my walk with Him. Perfectionism, which I have found is based on pride, and my addiction to fantasy, including the role-playing game Dungeons and Dragons, were sins that kept me from being close to the Lord. I should mention that my Dungeons and Dragons characters tended to do wicked things that I never would have done in real life, so there was a real problem there. I would play Dungeons and Dragons on Saturday evenings, then feel convicted when I went to church on Sunday, but I repeatedly told myself, "It's just a game." You see, God is perfect and holy. He hates sin. That's why He sent His son, Jesus Christ, to die on the cross as a sacrifice for our sins. I knew this and had asked Jesus to be my Savior and Lord, but I was still holding on to my sins.

Tremendous difficulty hit our family during my first year of college at Purdue in West Lafayette, Indiana. My dad and my brother were both diagnosed with cancer the same year, my dad with cancer of the tongue and my brother with Ewing's sarcoma in his chest. It was difficult for me to bear not being with them, since, living a three-hour drive away from home, I could not visit my family as often as I would have liked. When I did visit, I had some good talks with my dad. I know my dad found it much harder having a son with cancer than having cancer himself. I waited with him one day while my brother had a radiation treatment, and we discussed why the Lord allows suffering. I think, however, that whole thing was most difficult for my mother. Imagine what it would be like to have your husband and son come down with cancer at about the same time. When I look back, I can remember my mother's fortitude, and I know that the Lord was helping her through that trial. The Lord, being faithful, carried us all through it. In fact, a nurse shared with my family the poem, "Footprints in the Sand," by Mary Stevenson. It meant a lot to us, and, later, I made and framed a cross-stitch of the poem, which now hangs in my mother's bedroom. We prayed and believed that God would heal my dad and my brother, and He did miracles in their lives!

I started off as an aerospace engineering major in college, but, during my junior year at Purdue, I changed to an interdisciplinary engineering program. I combined aerospace engineering with biology, human factors engineering, organic chemistry and biochemistry in order to be prepared to work in manned spaceflight.

After college, I served in the Air Force in the Manned Spaceflight System Program Office at what was then called Los Angeles Air Force Station, now Los Angeles Air Force Base. We provided USAF astronauts with their training and researched methods and equipment for better servicing of satellites on-orbit. During one of our in-processing briefings, I had a big argument with a good-looking lieutenant named Dan. Little did I realize how significant that conversation would be.

After living in an apartment under less than desirable conditions for a while, I found a fellow female Air Force officer who, like me, wanted to share a house. My new roommate, Lori, and I found a cute little house in Torrance with avocado and lime trees in the back yard. It was delightful. I especially liked having laundry facilities right there in my house. Lori was also a Christian and was concerned about my addiction to fantasy books and Dungeons and Dragons. I wasn't actually playing Dungeons and Dragons any longer, but that was only because I hadn't found anyone with which to play. She prayed for me and encouraged me to get to know the Lord better.

Several months after Lori and I moved into our house, my dad had another bout with cancer. We prayed, my faith grew, and again God helped my family and me through it, and, amazingly, once again, my dad recovered, but this time most of his tongue was removed. Even with many weeks of therapy, it was very difficult for him to speak and eat after that; however, he did not complain but suffered patiently.

On January 28, 1986, the folks in my office gathered in front of closed circuit NASA TV to watch the launch of the space shuttle, "Challenger." We were all stunned as we watched the destruction of the orbiter shortly after launch. Our boss called us from Kennedy Space Center and told us to go home. After a few months, I was transferred to the Medium Launch Vehicle System Program Office (SPO). The Air Force was going to have to find another way to put its satellites on-orbit and needed to increase manpower on expendable launch vehicles.

I arrived in the Medium Launch Vehicle SPO just as they were preparing for a source selection to find a medium sized launch vehicle to put the Global Positioning System (GPS) on-orbit. After helping with the source selection, I was given Air Force oversight of the solid rocket motors and ordnance for the new Delta II launch vehicle. I also found myself working with that lieutenant I had argued with during in-processing. I found out that his name was Dan Runkle, and at this point, he was a captain. I apologized to him, as I recognized I had not had all my facts straight, and he was impressed by that. We also found out that we were both Christians.

As I came to know Dan better, he, like my roommate, was concerned about my affinity for fantasy and Dungeons and Dragons. The Lord used Matthew 5:21-28 to convict me of the sin in my life as I realized that playing at doing things that are wrong is very much like actually doing those things. I got rid of my fantasy books, threw away my Dungeons and Dragons book and dice, and began to grow in the Lord in a way I had not previously experienced. The difference real repentance made was amazing. I was hungry for God's Word, as I hadn't been in years.

My parents were coming to visit me during the summer of 1987 and, it so happened that my neighbor, who had been an executive with Goodyear, gave me four tickets to ride the Goodyear blimp. That does not happen every day, and I wanted to share the ride with someone who would really appreciate it. Of course, my parents and I made three, but who would be the fourth? I thought about all my friends and finally decided that my friend, Dan, from work would probably enjoy it the most, so I invited him. We had a wonderful time and my folks invited him out to dinner afterward. Before the evening was over, my folks had also invited Dan to go sightseeing with us the next day. My parents were planning to drive up the coast to San Francisco and fly home, and they left a couple of days after our sightseeing excursion. Upon their arrival home, mom called and asked how serious Dan and I were. I told her, "Mom, we're just friends. It was *your* idea to invite him to dinner and then to go sightseeing with us." Mom replied, "Well, he's the one."

I married my wonderful husband, Dan, in 1988 and was amazed at how the Lord worked in our relationship. It was in large part our love for the Lord that had brought us together and we had prayed and talked about the Lord on our dates. It was apparent not only to my parents, but to my brother and sister also, that Dan was "the one." Soon after we were married, Dan took a position as Assistant Professor of Aerospace Studies in the Air Force ROTC detachment at Louisiana State University in Baton Rouge. I left the Air Force, and we both began graduate studies at LSU. I had become very interested in materials science during my tenure in the Air Force and did my research in composite materials. During that time, the Lord began to show me that my perfectionism was rooted in pride and a lack of reliance on Him. When I began to let go of the perfectionism, I felt a freedom and confidence I had never known before. I'm definitely still a work in progress in this regard and I relapse into it on occasion, but the Lord has brought me a long way.

After graduate school, Dan decided to leave the Air Force, and we found work at a small metallurgical failure analysis firm in Baton Rouge. It had been a bit of a stretch financially for them to hire both of us, and we soon saw that we were going to need to find other work. We hadn't wanted to leave Baton Rouge, but necessity was going to dictate a move. We found jobs together at Lockheed Martin Michoud Assembly Facility in New Orleans and moved to Picayune, Mississippi. Michoud Assembly Facility (MAF) has a rich history. The location was originally a sugar cane plantation and refinery, but was made into a large aircraft manufacturing facility during World War II. In the 1960's, Saturn boosters were made there and, in the 1970s, production began on the space shuttle external tank, which Michoud was still producing when we worked there. Dan worked in stress analysis, and I worked in the materials group. I was able to do some projects involving composite materials, but I mainly worked with aluminum. It dawned on me during that time that I was, in a way, following in the footsteps of both of my grandfathers, one of whom had worked in the lead and zinc mining industry of southwestern Wisconsin, while the other had been a tool-and-die maker.

I enjoyed graduate school and my work at Lockheed Martin, but Dan and I also wanted to have children, and that would take a little longer than we thought it would. Two miscarriages, one while I was in graduate school and the second shortly after we started working for Lockheed Martin, taught me more about faith in my Lord, and I was especially grateful for my sister's prayers and encouragement when I was struggling after the second one. Sooner than should have been physically possible, I was pregnant again! This time, with the help of a terrific OB/Gyn, Dr. Caire, who specialized in helping women who had multiple miscarriages, I gave birth to our oldest, Sarah, in July of 1996. When she was born, she had such a healthy cry that Dr. Caire, quoting Psalm 150, exclaimed, "Let everything that has breath praise the Lord, and she certainly has breath!"

In Picayune, we were renovating what we thought was our 75-year-old dream home. We found a church and Dan really enjoyed connecting with the men there; however, I had trouble fitting in. The house we were living in and renovating contained lead-based paint, a concern that became an obsession for me after Sarah was born. At the same time, my dad's health, which had been slowly declining over several years, began to fail. I wanted so badly to be closer to home, to be near my folks and help my mom. I barely slept, I had panic attacks almost daily, and I had great difficulty focusing at work. I thought I was losing my mind. Many days all I could pray was "Help," and, as my dad's health declined, my daily prayer became, "Lord, please let us move closer to home." Oh how I wanted to be out of that house and closer to home! During that hard year, God was holding on to me, even though I couldn't often feel it, and He was using all that was happening to build my faith in Him.

In March of that year, my mom called me to tell me that my Dad's passing was imminent and said I should get there right away, so I traveled up to Palatine, Illinois. My dad had twice walked through cancer of the tongue. Because of the treatment for it, he had had great difficulty eating and talking. His health had been slowly failing for about ten years, and he was dying. Sarah was eight months old, and I took her with me. My dad was at home on hospice care. One of the darkest nights of my life, was Wednesday, March 5, 1997, but, in the midst of the darkness of that night, God spoke to me.

That night, I was upstairs in my old bedroom at my parent's house, and my dad was downstairs in the family room in a hospital bed. My wise, gentle, humble father was leaving us. I knew that, but I didn't. Part of me knew Dad was dying, and part of me wouldn't accept it. Sarah and I both had colds, and I was afraid we might be making him more ill. In addition, I only had a limited amount of time off work and I was afraid I would have to go back to Picayune too soon. I wanted to be there when he passed away. I cried out to the Lord in despair, "Am I here at the right time? Sarah and I both have colds. What if Dad catches the cold and gets worse? I have to go back to work in a few days, and what if Mom needs me and I can't get back?" I know that what I said didn't really make sense. I wasn't thinking straight. I had been worried about Dad, about the lead-based paint in our house, about my new daughter. I had been having difficulty sleeping, having panic attacks, struggling with depression. It was a very difficult time. As I prayed, there were quiet words in my mind, and I believe the Holy Spirit was speaking to me. He said, "You're here at the right time. I've heard your mother's prayers. I'm taking him Friday."

That Friday, my dad passed away, but I was so comforted, knowing that God was in control. He had told me that it would happen and it did. I can't tell you how much it encouraged me to know that this was part of the Lord's plan for my dad, and I was amazed by the fact that the God who created the whole universe would bend down and tell one of His children about His plan. I've talked with many friends who have had similar experiences. God speaks to His children! I don't think God speaks to us like that very often, but, when He does, I think it's because He knows that we are desperate to hear from Him.

I still wanted to be closer to home, to help Mom through her grief. God is so faithful, and I am still amazed at how He answered that prayer! He led my husband to apply for a seminary education. Before I knew it, my husband had been accepted to Trinity Evangelical Divinity School in Deerfield, IL. The Lord confirmed this choice in many ways. I got a job at an aluminum mill in McCook, IL without an interview, since they knew me, as they were one of our suppliers at Lockheed Martin. The Lord even miraculously provided the exact amount of the funds we needed for Dan to resign and finish the house we were renovating so we could sell it. My dad had passed away in March and, by August, we were living just blocks from my mom. I had never dreamed that the Lord would move me that close to home.

While living in Palatine, we had two more children, Grace and Jacob. Grace's birth was quite easy. When we arrived at the hospital, there was not even time to finish putting in the epidural needle before I needed to push. Two pushes and she was out! The doctor barely arrived in time to catch her. However, when my youngest, Jacob, was being born, things were a bit more difficult. Jacob's heart rate plummeted with every contraction and my physician began preparing for an emergency C-section. We later discovered that the umbilical cord had been wrapped around his neck. My husband asked the doctor if he would mind if he prayed aloud. Our doctor replied, "Please do." As soon as Dan finished praying, the doctor had me change position, and a few minutes later, Jacob was safely born. I believe that was no coincidence! It was God's Providence in our lives.

During the years in Palatine, Dan completed seminary, the Lord gave me great success at work, our kids were able to spend lots of time with Grandma, and life was good. The Lord was continuing to work with me, stretching me and increasing my faith in Him. Life was still stressful, and I never had as much time with the Lord as I felt I should, but the future looked very bright.

Then Dan got his first pastorate in Cape Girardeau, MO. We realized rather quickly that we had walked into a messy situation. We didn't realize it ahead of time, but the church had had a lot of conflict and had split five times in about 15 years. It was becoming clear that, short of a major change of heart on the part of some key people, another church split was inevitable.

In the midst of all the conflict, we found out I had breast cancer. Initially, my diagnosis was ductile carcinoma in situ or DCIS, which meant that the cancer was only in the milk ducts and not in surrounding tissue. DCIS is also referred to as stage zero cancer, since it is not invasive. I wanted to be certain about my diagnosis, so I decided to go to St. Louis for a second opinion. The oncologist I saw there told me the cancer *was* invasive.

Initially, it was very hard for me to face this news. I felt so guilty. Guilt is, apparently, a common reaction to a cancer diagnosis. I cried and prayed. I cried out to the Lord for His encouragement, but had trouble finding it at first. As folks prayed for me, I felt the joy of the Lord return. Then I would again become distressed. I had been concerned before my diagnosis that there wasn't much depth to my repentance, that I didn't really see how bad my sins were to the Lord. My quiet times were often short and perfunctory. In her book, *What Happens When God Answers Prayer*, Evelyn Cristensen compares sin to a cancer. It occurred to me that what was going on in my body was a mirror of the soul. The deliverance I needed most of all was deliverance from sin! In the midst of my period of repentance, First Peter 4:1 caught my eye. "Therefore, since Christ suffered for us in the flesh, arm yourselves also with the same mind, for he who has suffered in the flesh has ceased from sin, that he no longer should live the rest of his time in the flesh for the lusts of men, but for the will of God." (1 Pet. 4:1, NKJV)   Could it be, I thought, that this experience would help me to be more holy? That was my heart's desire. In fact, I had been yearning and praying for this very thing for months. However, I was frustrated in my efforts, because I couldn't do it. I wanted to have a meaningful daily quiet time. I wanted to be a better wife and mother. I wanted to be a truer friend. I was so unhappy with my efforts. I'm sure many people feel the same way.

After thinking about having invasive cancer for a couple of days, I thought about the advice I had received from my mother-in-law's best friend, Olga. She was already walking through fourth stage breast cancer and had told me to request a PET (positron emission tomography) scan to see if the cancer had spread to other parts of my body.   A PET scan is an imaging test that uses a radioactive tracer attached to glucose molecules. Since cancer cells metabolize more quickly than normal cells, they take up the glucose more quickly. The tracer gets concentrated in the cancer cells and releases positrons as it decays.   These positrons are detected by the equipment, showing where the cancer cells are located in the body. The results of the scan were not what I wanted to hear. The cancer had already spread to about nine lymph nodes, my thyroid gland, and my sternum.

As I lived through this very difficult year, the Lord spoke into my life, through His Word, the Holy Spirit, and the voices of friends. The lessons I learned that year are the subject of this book. It is my fervent hope that, as you read, you will see Jesus, hear His voice, believe His word, and trust Him with everything. He is the only one worthy of all of our trust and love.

Jane Runkle

2 GOD SPEAKS

I was on a business trip in Alabama, when I received the phone call from my oncologist's office with the results of the PET scan. I was doing some consulting work with Lockheed Martin and was visiting Marshall Spaceflight Center. It was upsetting being away from home and getting the news that the cancer had not only spread, but also appeared to be in a bone. I knew that oncologists consider it almost impossible to cure bone metastases. I couldn't concentrate on the meeting and slipped out a couple of times to call my husband. That evening, when I got to my hotel room, I called my sister, Laura, as well. My husband and my sister were very encouraging, as I spoke with them over the phone. Laura prayed for me words from scripture including words from Isaiah 40, Psalm 23, and Psalm 91. In fact, over the course of the next few weeks, three different people prayed Psalm 23 for me. What promises we have in God's Word! Of course, I wanted Him to heal me, but I was asking all along for Him to show me what He was doing with me. You must understand that I didn't go looking for what I wanted to hear. I asked the Lord to speak to me through His word and He directed me to the scripture promises He had for me at that time.

When I found out the cancer was in my sternum, I asked the Lord what I should read, as I often do. He told me to keep reading where I was reading. I was reading Ezekiel and was on Ezekiel 37 that day. Ezekiel was writing to the southern kingdom of Judah in the years leading up to and during the Babylonian captivity. He wrote about the coming destruction of Jerusalem by the Babylonians. In Ezekiel 37, he wrote about the restoration of Israel from spiritual death.

The hand of the LORD came upon me and brought me out in the Spirit of the LORD, and set me down in the midst of the valley; and it was full of bones. ²Then He caused me to pass by them all around, and behold, there were very many in the open valley; and indeed they were very dry. ³And He said to me, "Son of man, can these bones live?"

So I answered, "O Lord GOD, You know."

⁴Again He said to me, "Prophesy to these bones, and say to them, 'O dry bones, hear the word of the LORD! ⁵Thus says the Lord GOD to these bones: "Surely I will cause breath to enter into you, and you shall live. ⁶I will put sinews on you and bring flesh upon you, cover you with skin and put breath in you; and you shall live. Then you shall know that I am the LORD."'"

⁷So I prophesied as I was commanded; and as I prophesied, there was a noise, and suddenly a rattling; and the bones came together, bone to bone. ⁸Indeed, as I looked, the sinews and the flesh came upon them, and the skin covered them over; but there was no breath in them.

⁹Also He said to me, "Prophesy to the breath, prophesy, son of man, and say to the breath, 'Thus says the Lord GOD: "Come from the four winds, O breath, and breathe on these slain, that they may live."'" ¹⁰So I prophesied as He commanded me, and breath came into them, and they lived, and stood upon their feet, an exceedingly great army.

¹¹Then He said to me, "Son of man, these bones are the whole house of Israel. They indeed say, 'Our bones are dry, our hope is lost, and we ourselves are cut off!' ¹²Therefore prophesy and say to them, 'Thus says the Lord GOD: "Behold, O My people, I will open your graves and cause you to come up from your graves, and bring you into the land of Israel. [13] Then you shall know that I am the LORD, when I have opened your graves, O My people, and brought you up from your graves. [14] I will put My Spirit in you, and you shall live, and I will place you in your own land. Then you shall know that I, the LORD, have spoken it and performed it," says the LORD."(Exodus 37:1-14, NKJV)

Now I recognize that this passage is about Israel and about spiritual life. However, I believe the Lord was using it to remind me that He is the giver of life, both spiritual and physical. I also realize that this was a vision, not an actual occurrence; however, the point is that the Lord is able to make dry bones live and cause dead spirits to revive. In light of that then, I rejoiced. "Oh Lord," I responded, "if you can bring those bones to life, you can bring life to this bone!" I knew those words were a promise from the Lord to me.

After receiving the results of the scan, I was referred to a medical oncologist who didn't give me much hope. In fact, he wasn't even going to *try* to cure me. I was so frightened when I first went to this doctor's office that I can't even adequately describe to you the cold feeling of dread that came over me when I walked in. I wanted to run away. Thank the Lord; there was a man there who was with his wife and father-in-law, who was being treated for cancer. The man was a Baptist deacon, who spoke enthusiastically about his faith in our Lord and told me not to give up, because I had a story to tell. His wife and I prayed together. What a blessing! The fear left, and I was able to go into the oncologist's office full of peace, joy and confidence from the Lord. It was a good thing, because the oncologist's fellow, who I saw that day, didn't seem to understand that I was going to get well. She said I was just to have a Lupron shot to kill my ovaries and Arimidex to remove the estrogen and progesterone from my system. This didn't seem right to me, but I agreed to try it and wait until the next month to talk with the oncologist.

That night, my women's prayer group anointed me with oil and prayed for my healing, especially for my breastbone. The Lord kept on giving me promises from His word. Specifically, He showed me that I was "walking *through* the valley of the *shadow* of death" (Psalm 23:4), walking through and it was just a shadow. In fact, three different people prayed those words from Psalm 23 for me. The Lord also told me through His word that I "would see the goodness of the Lord in the land of the living" (Psalm 27:13), and that "with long life I will satisfy him and show him My salvation." (Psalm 91:16)

By this time, April of 2004, Dan had resigned from his pastorate, and we had joined Lynwood Baptist Church, a church in Cape Girardeau that we loved. It had been our support church. The kids had gone to Mothers' Day Out there, I had attended Precept Bible Studies there, and Dan had become good friends with the pastor, Derek Staples, through the Cape Girardeau Ministerial Alliance.

Friends Bill and Lynn Suhre from our previous church began attending Lynwood around the same time and continued to be an encouragement to us. Bill had been an elder and Lynn had been the secretary of the church Dan had pastored. We continued to get together with Carl and Shirley Archer, who were also dear friends from our former church. Carl and Shirley would invite us over for chicken wings, and Carl's keen sense of humor often buoyed us up. I'll never forget how Carl taught Jacob "baby five." Carl would say "baby five" to Jacob, and Jacob would gently jab his little index finger into Carl's palm, just as Carl had shown him.

I had gotten the results of the PET scan just a couple of weeks before joining Lynwood and was still reeling from the change in my diagnosis from stage 0 to stage 4, when three people from our new church showed up at our front door. One of the ladies, Joey Crosnoe, read 2 Chronicles, chapter 20, to us.

20 *It happened after this that the people of Moab with the people of Ammon, and others with them besides the Ammonites, came to battle* *against Jehoshaphat.* ² *Then some came and told Jehoshaphat, saying, "A great multitude is coming against you from beyond the sea, from Syria; and they are in Hazazon Tamar" (which is En Gedi).* ³ *And Jehoshaphat feared, and set himself to seek the LORD, and proclaimed a fast throughout all Judah.* ⁴ *So Judah gathered together to ask help from the LORD; and from all the cities of Judah they came to seek the LORD.*

⁵ *Then Jehoshaphat stood in the assembly of Judah and Jerusalem, in the house of the LORD, before the new court,* ⁶ *and said: "O LORD God of our fathers, are You not God in heaven, and do You not rule over all the kingdoms of the nations, and in Your hand is there not power and might, so that no one is able to withstand You?* ⁷ *Are You not our God, who drove out the inhabitants of this land before Your people Israel, and gave it to the descendants of Abraham Your friend forever?* ⁸ *And they dwell in it, and have built You a sanctuary in it for Your name, saying,* ⁹ *'If disaster comes upon us—sword, judgment, pestilence, or famine—we will stand before this temple and in Your presence (for Your name is in this temple), and cry out to You in our affliction, and You will hear and save.'* ¹⁰ *And now, here are the people of Ammon, Moab, and Mount Seir—whom You would not let Israel invade when they came out of the land of Egypt, but they turned from them and did not destroy them—* ¹¹ *here they are, rewarding us by coming to throw us out of Your possession which You have given us to inherit.* ¹² *O our God, will You not judge them? For we have no power against this great multitude that is coming against us; nor do we know what to do, but our eyes are upon You."*

¹³ *Now all Judah, with their little ones, their wives, and their children, stood before the LORD.* ¹⁴ *Then the Spirit of the LORD came upon Jahaziel the son of Zechariah, the son of Benaiah, the son of Jeiel, the son of Mattaniah, a Levite of the sons of Asaph, in the midst of the assembly.* ¹⁵ *And he said, "Listen, all you of Judah and you inhabitants of Jerusalem, and you, King Jehoshaphat! Thus says the LORD to you: 'Do not be afraid nor dismayed because of this great multitude, for the battle is not yours, but God's.* ¹⁶ *Tomorrow go down against them. They*

will surely come up by the Ascent of Ziz, and you will find them at the end of the brook before the Wilderness of Jeruel.[17] You will not need to fight in this battle. Position yourselves, stand still and see the salvation of the LORD, who is with you, O Judah and Jerusalem!' Do not fear or be dismayed; tomorrow go out against them, for the LORD is with you." [18] And Jehoshaphat bowed his head with his face to the ground, and all Judah and the inhabitants of Jerusalem bowed before the LORD, worshiping the LORD. [19] Then the Levites of the children of the Kohathites and of the children of the Korahites stood up to praise the LORD God of Israel with voices loud and high. [20] So they rose early in the morning and went out into the Wilderness of Tekoa; and as they went out, Jehoshaphat stood and said, "Hear me, O Judah and you inhabitants of Jerusalem: Believe in the LORD your God, and you shall be established; believe His prophets, and you shall prosper." [21] And when he had consulted with the people, he appointed those who should sing to the LORD, and who should praise the beauty of holiness, as they went out before the army and were saying:

"Praise the LORD,

For His mercy endures forever."

[22] Now when they began to sing and to praise, the LORD set ambushes against the people of Ammon, Moab, and Mount Seir, who had come against Judah; and they were defeated. [23] For the people of Ammon and Moab stood up against the inhabitants of Mount Seir to utterly kill and destroy them. And when they had made an end of the inhabitants of Seir, they helped to destroy one another. [24] So when Judah came to a place overlooking the wilderness, they looked toward the multitude; and there were their dead bodies, fallen on the earth. No one had escaped. (2 Chronicles 20:1-24, NKJV)

God spoke to His people. I just love this passage, and am so thankful Joey chose to read it to us to encourage us that day! Here is what I think is so significant. First, King Jehoshaphat acknowledged to the Lord that Israel was powerless against their enemy, and he focused on the Lord and His promises. I believe King Jehoshaphat and, indeed, Israel prayed expecting God to speak to them! Second, the Lord answered! He said that the battle was not theirs, but it was His. In a sermon series, Dr. Carroll Marr of Southcliff Baptist Church in Fort Worth, Texas described the covenant God has made with us. He explained that, in ancient times, when people entered into a covenant with one another, one of the things they did was to exchange robes, and, in so doing, they exchanged identities. Likewise, God gave Israel and us a new identity as His people. They also exchanged swords, which was an exchange of enemies. Our enemies are now God's and His enemy is now ours. He will take care of our enemies for us and, since His enemy was already defeated at the cross, we have no enemy to fear. That's why the battle was His to fight for Israel. What did they need to do? First, they had to position themselves. Let's apply this to our lives. How do we position ourselves? I believe our responsibility is to be obedient, to be where God wants us to be, doing what He wants us to do. We need to put on His armor (Ephesians 6:10-20). We need to pray. We need to be humbly bowed before Him. Secondly, they were to stand still and see the victory of the Lord. Likewise, we are to stand and watch the Lord win the victory. This is true in every area of our lives.

However, what does it mean to stand? Well, I think Jehoshaphat answered that question very well. He said to believe in God and to believe God; that is, to believe what He has said through the prophets. Thus, standing means to stand on His word, to stand on His promises, and to praise the Lord. Notice that the people of Israel praised the Lord before they saw the victory. The words used here for praise are significant. The word for sing is *rinnah* and its meaning includes shouting and rejoicing in victory. The word for praise is *tehillah*, and it means songs of admiration and celebration. The people were literally celebrating the victory God promised before they saw it. Had the victory happened yet? No, it hadn't, but they believed God and stepped out in faith. When He tells us something, we believe Him, we praise Him, and we celebrate what He has promised! That is how we stand. That is faith. We know that, "without faith it is impossible to please Him..." (Hebrews 11:6, NKJV) I believe that conversely, this kind of faith must please Him. In *The Peace and Power of Knowing God's Name*, Kay Arthur talks about God Almighty, El Shaddai, "who delights to succor His people,... who delights to comfort His children, ... who longs to hold and protect His own." (Arthur, p. 41) And He has promised to do that. He just wants us to believe Him.

Finally, in verse 17, God, through Jahaziel, said that Israel would see the salvation of the Lord. We must be on the lookout. We dare not miss what God is doing around us. We must be watchful for His blessings so we can praise Him. We must be watchful for His discipline so we, like Ezekiel, can be warned and warn others. We must be watchful for His work so we can join Him in it. (Blackaby)

One day, the Lord led me to read Psalm 30, and I read it over and over during those months. It remains one of my favorite scripture passages. "O Lord, my God, I cried out to You And You healed me…. Weeping may endure for a night, But joy comes in the morning...." (Psalm 30:2,5, NKJV) Many a night I wept, and many a morning I was filled with joy, as the Lord gave me new promises from His Word. "You have turned for me my mourning into dancing… O Lord my God, I will give thanks to You forever." (Psalm 30:11-12, NKJV) My mourning was being turned into dancing on a day by day basis, as I trusted the Lord more and more.

I was greatly encouraged by the Lord, but outward circumstances were still rather discouraging. I was concerned that the Lupron shot hadn't worked. I went back to the oncologist's office after a month and he said that I just needed to stay on the Arimidex until it stopped working and then they'd give me something else until that stopped working. I asked about my prognosis and he said, "Normally I'd say you'd have three to four years, but I think you'll live longer than that." I said, "I have a two year old. I need twenty years." I asked about chemo and he said he didn't want to add that toxicity to me. I thought, "Add it to what?" I wondered if he had me confused with another patient, since I had never had chemotherapy before.

I went home that day and called my friend, Jean Seres, who also led our women's prayer group. We wept and prayed. I related to her that I told the doctor I knew the Lord was healing me. Jean responded, "Fear knocked at the door, faith answered, and there was no one there." The next day, I prayed some more. I remembered the assurance I had received from the Lord. He had told me the He would never leave me nor forsake me. (Deut. 31:6) He had told me to stand and watch what He would do, and I dearly wanted to obey!

When I prayed that day, I said, "Lord, I believe you are going to heal me. Please show me if I should stick with this doctor or be more proactive." The next morning, my husband said to me (and I think it was the first thing he said to me that day), "We need to check into MD Anderson." That was on Saturday, so I had to wait through the rest of the weekend before I could call, and I waited anxiously but expectantly.

That Monday, I called MD Anderson, which is the best cancer hospital in the US and probably in the world, to find out if they might be able to help me. The first person I spoke to said I needed to stay on my current treatment and call back in a month. I realized that they probably were accustomed to patients being referred by their physicians, so this was probably an unusual situation for the young woman to whom I spoke. However, the thought that ran through my mind was, "That is *not* the right answer," so I asked to speak to her supervisor. She readily acquiesced and was very kind to put her superior on the phone. After I explained everything that had happened and sent them all of the information I had, the supervisor said she thought they needed to try to help me, and that she would look into what they could do. By the end of the day, I was speaking with the Administrative Director of the Breast Center, who told me that I was not on the right treatment, but that there was a doctor who was *excited* about the treatment he could offer me. She insisted that I try to get there by the next Monday. People don't usually get appointments that quickly! "Wow," I thought, "That's an answer to prayer." I felt the Lord was confirming to me that He wanted me to go there.

We planned to drive to MD Anderson in Houston, TX. Since my husband had resigned his pastorate, we didn't have money to fly. However, when our pastor at Lynwood heard from Lynn Suhre that we were going to drive from Cape Girardeau to Houston, he was concerned that the trip would be too exhausting for us and decided to have the church to buy our plane tickets. In addition, my husband's brother paid for our hotel stay. It turned out that this was just the beginning of the financial provision the Lord would send us.

The Lord also provided us with help in keeping the children while we were in Houston. Since we had no relatives nearby, we were going to have to ask friends to take the kids. We didn't want to ask one family to keep all three kids for five days; that seemed like too great a burden, so we planned to ask three families to keep one child each. The goal was to choose people our kids knew well. The first person we asked was Sandy South, our son's teacher in the preschool program at Lynwood, and her response was that, not only would she keep Jacob for us, but she would keep all three of our kids. She insisted, saying that it would not be good for them to be separated at such a time. We were thrilled. We knew she would take good care of our kids, and we didn't worry about them while we were in Houston.

When we arrived at the airport in Houston, we were met by a woman named Joy Godby. Now, Joy was the sister-in-law of a lady at our church, who had arranged for us to meet. Joy, a pastor's wife, was working in the Radiation Oncology Business Office at MD Anderson. She knew MD Anderson up and down and showed us around. She also led a Bible Study at MD Anderson, which I visited several times when I was there for appointments. She seemed to me to be joy personified, and when I think about my favorite Psalm, Psalm 30, she always comes to mind.

That first week at MD Anderson was long and difficult. I was in and out of exam rooms and tests for about four days. However, there was a refreshing atmosphere of hope there, which I had not experienced anywhere else. I saw scripture verses on the walls in various places, and the nurses and technicians I met were so cheerful and upbeat, I couldn't help but feel that all would be well. The patients made jokes with each other. That helped. We pretended that the barium milkshakes were delicious and, in fact, they did come in more than one flavor. It was fun to get to choose. One patient told me that the reason we were called patients was because that's what we had to be - patient! I found, however, that the waits were worth it!

After many tests and a multidisciplinary tumor conference, my oncologist, Dr. Booser, said, "We're going to work toward a cure." What great words to hear! He also told me that my treatment was not a standard treatment, and I later learned that, unlike most cancer centers, MD Anderson is able to customize care including the use of novel treatment strategies. (Breast Cancer Treatment) There was a lot ahead of me, however. He said I would start chemotherapy. I asked him, "When?" He answered, "Tonight." That was at around 4:30 in the afternoon on May 20, 2004. I finished my first treatment at about 1:30 the next morning!

The next day, Dan and I flew home. At first, I was quite wired from the steroid they gave me. I didn't expect to have that kind of energy; however, when the steroid wore off, I was unbelievably tired. Shortly after we came home, my older daughter, Sarah, came down with gastroenteritis. Dan took care of her, so that I wouldn't get sick, and the next day, I went to my prayer group meeting. Jean, the group leader, taught us a song by Stephen Hurd based on 2 Timothy 1:7, which says, "For God has not given us a spirit of fear, but of power and of love and of a sound mind."

That night, I began to feel very ill, started vomiting and had diarrhea. I had never been so sick in all my life. It seemed like it went on for hours non-stop. My husband called our deacon from church, Steve Smith, and he and his wife, Susie, came over right away. I don't recall what time it was, but it was very late. I was lying in bed at one point, hearing their voices in the next room as they discussed what to do. I thought, "I'm going to have to go to the hospital," and I was right. Dan took me to the hospital, and Steve and Susie stayed with the kids.

I was admitted, severely dehydrated and dangerously neutropenic. My compromised immune system couldn't fight the virus. I was so weak, I couldn't sit up, and, when I was taken for a chest x-ray, it was all I could do to stay in the wheelchair. I was rather frightened, but the song Jean had taught me from 2 Timothy 1:7 ran over and over in my head. I realized I did not need to be afraid, because God has given me a spirit of power and of love and of a sound mind. Although I had barely been able to stay in the wheelchair, somehow, by God's grace, I was able to stand for the chest x-ray.

I ended up staying in the hospital for about four days. The first nurse I had didn't really know what to do with a neutropenic patient. I was then assigned an oncology nurse who insisted on quarantining me. She told my husband that I could die, and he became greatly concerned. I couldn't eat at all for the first two days. They kept bringing me food, and I couldn't even look at it. Finally, I began to improve, and my nurse told me that, if I ate my entire dinner, I could have ice cream. That motivated me, and I finally ate.

The next day, I was released and Dan drove over to pick me up, but there were severe storms and a tornado warning in effect when we were ready to leave. We had to take cover in the hallway of the hospital until the storm passed, and then, finally, I was allowed to go home. It was May 29, my birthday. The kids had had fun with Steve and Susie, who also watched them that day, so Dan could get me from the hospital, and I was so grateful for their help!

After my hospital stay, Dan was very concerned about any exposure to germs. I had to wear a mask when I went out. Once I started getting Neulasta to build up my white blood cells and Procrit to build up my red blood cells, I was finally able to convince him to let me go without a mask. He had taken that oncology nurses' warning very seriously. On June 27, I went to church without the mask, and it felt so good!

As Dr. Booser had said, my treatment was not a standard treatment for breast cancer. Since the cancer was HER-2 positive, I received Herceptin every week. Then every third week, I would also get Carboplatin and Taxotere. At that time, Taxotere was a standard chemotherapy for breast cancer, but Carboplatin was usually used for lung cancer. When I returned to MD Anderson June 10 for my second treatment, Dr. Booser noted that he already could no longer feel any nodules on my thyroid gland. He also noticed significant improvement in my breast. He seemed pleased, and I was thrilled. The chemotherapy was working!

I ended up having a total of eleven three-week rounds of treatment. I received some of my chemotherapy at MD Anderson; however, since we lived in Missouri, Dr. Booser referred me to an oncologist near our home, Dr. Lyss, at Ste. Genevieve County Memorial Hospital.

In Dr. Lyss' examining room, I first noticed the calendar with scripture verses for every month. The one for June was, "Let everything that has breath, praise the Lord!" (Psalm 150:6) That was encouraging to me, since it was the verse my obstetrician quoted when our older daughter, Sarah, was born. I had been grumpy all morning, and had had to apologize to Dan repeatedly. Dan was not angry with me, but was kind and patient. I realized, while I waited for Dr. Lyss that I was afraid he would say something discouraging to me, like the doctor at the other cancer center had. However, I prayed and saw the calendar, and the Lord gave me His peace.

Cancer patients must often feel guilty about having cancer. I know I did. I felt very responsible for what my family had to endure. I figured it must have been my poor diet, lack of exercise, excessive worry, sins in my life, etc. I did spend a lot of time repenting that first month, and it was good for me to do that. When the Lord has our attention as He had mine, it is very important to repent, and there were certainly things the Lord wanted to change in my life. Apparently, Dr. Lyss also knew that this was a common issue for cancer patients, because, the first time I met him, he leaned forward in his chair, got almost nose-to-nose with me, looked me right in the eyes, and said, "This is not your fault. You did nothing to deserve this." WOW! What an encouraging thing for a physician to say. I realized that the Lord had indeed forgiven my sins and was going to use this cancer for good, perhaps not only in my life but in the lives of those close to me, as well, but Dr. Lyss' words were like rain on parched ground. What a blessing to have, not just my friends, but also my physician, tell me this. I tear up even today, when I think about it.

I was also quite worried during those first few months about something else. If the Lord should decide to take me home, I wondered, how would my children grow up without their mother? How would my husband manage? It was a very real concern to me. I was thankful when, after weeks of wrestling with this thought, the Lord brought me to the place where I was able to put those children in His hands. I knew, beyond any doubt, that, since He loved them more than I did, He could certainly take better care of them than I could. I knew He could give my husband the strength he needed to raise them without me.

For about 3 months, I was up during the night almost every night crying out to the Lord in desperation. During those weeks after my diagnosis, the Lord led me in turning over area after area of my life to Him. Then, one morning in June, after I'd been on chemo about a month, I awoke filled with joy. I don't mean a "before I got cancer" kind of joy. I mean the "I don't know if I've ever had this in my life" kind of joy. I thought to myself, "You've got 4th stage cancer. You have three little kids, and you're going through chemo. You're supposed to be depressed. Where did all this joy come from?" Of course, I knew. It was from the Lord.

Chemotherapy was hard, of course, but the Lord was with me. The first week I was terribly tired, and it wasn't like any kind of fatigue I'd ever experienced. Sleep didn't really help. The second week, my mouth would hurt. At first, it wasn't so bad, but around the third treatment, it hurt so much I could barely eat. My mouth and my whole digestive tract felt raw. I would mash food and eat it cold, which would make it bearable, but it was still painful. Oatmeal felt like tacks in my mouth. I forgot to keep taking the dexamethasone, a steroid used to treat inflammation, after my third treatment, so my thumbs swelled and the skin on my hands became itchy and sore, then peeled. I wrote in my diary that I had learned my lesson about taking it very well.

Treatments continued with weeks one and two being really rough, but week three was always better. During week three, I'd almost feel normal, but too soon it would be time to begin all over again. I was also having frequent hot flashes, since I had been forced into early menopause by the Lupron shot. I didn't mind getting warm, but I didn't like being grumpy, and the hot flashes made me feel panicky and irritable. I found, however, that, as I abided more and more with the Lord through my cancer journey, that I was less and less irritable. It was God's grace given for that time. He gives grace as we need it, and, when we rest in Him, we will surely see Him at work in our lives.

I'll never forget how I could feel the chemotherapy make me well. Chemotherapy has a bad reputation in some circles, which I think is undeserved. After my second treatment, I recall being able to play in the yard with my 2-year-old son, moving as I hadn't been able to move in over a year. Before beginning treatment, I had felt decrepit, but, after only two chemotherapy treatments, I was starting to feel more youthful again. The chemotherapy was helping my body fight the cancer, and it needed the help. The Lord was using it to heal me; of that, I am quite certain.

Since Dan usually took me for my treatments and, since our children were small, we often went as a family. I think it probably helped the kids to be included, so that it wasn't all a mystery to them. In order to facilitate normalcy for all of us, we would often make my appointments in Ste. Genevieve an adventure. Sometimes we went to the swimming pool there and happily splashed about in that indoor playground. Sometimes we visited the library. We often stopped for ice cream before getting on the highway to drive home. Making it fun helped all of us not only to endure, but also to look forward to my treatments. Even today, Grace and Sarah remember how fun it was to visit Ste. Genevieve.

My sister and her husband, Todd, visited us right before my third treatment and were a huge encouragement to me. My sister, Laura prayed diligently for me throughout my year with cancer. When we pray diligently for one another, we are doing more than we often realize. "The effective, fervent prayer of a righteous man avails much." (James 1:5, NKJV) Todd and Laura took Sarah and Grace back home with them to northern Illinois to visit with them and my mom for two weeks. It was good for the girls' to get away, and enjoy their cousins, Grandma Daugherty, and their aunt and uncle.

During the girls' stay, my Grandma Perkins passed away, so the girls attended the funeral with my mother and my sister. I was glad they were there to represent our family. My husband was out of town, so Jacob and I were home by ourselves, and, since I could not drive that far, I was not able to attend the funeral. I admit I felt a bit sorry for myself. I really wanted to be there with my family. They would all be there - aunts, uncles and cousins, people I hadn't seen in years. My heart was there, however, and I wrote a poem. I realize the poem is not very good; however, I'll share it here, so you can get a little picture of my grandma, who was very dear to me.

Grandma Perkins' kitchen sure smelled good.
(With Grandma, you always knew where you stood).
After dinner, we'd walk to see the beaver dam,
And by the football field, where sat many a fan.
Grandma could play a mean badminton game,
But most importantly, she was called by Christ's name.
Yes, In Sunday school, she taught us a lot.
Using flannel graphs, she imparted wise thoughts,
And back when it wasn't the "in" thing to do,
In church, she would give us gum to chew.
Her sayings are famous, her passion Divine,
I thank the Lord for Grandma, and that she was mine.

Grandma lived in a small town in Wisconsin, the town where my mother grew up. My grandparents were godly people, who imparted a legacy of faith to our family. That side of my family hailed mainly from Cornwall, UK, and they were Methodist miners, hardworking, independent, witty, and forthright. How I loved visiting them. By the way, Grandma's kitchen often smelled good because of a pasty baking in the oven. YUM!

Grandma Perkins' passing marked for me the end of an era. My paternal grandparents had passed away years before, and Grandpa Perkins went to be with the Lord in 1998. My Uncle Fred, my mom's youngest brother and a Primitive Methodist pastor, had preached at his funeral and shared, at that time, about how Grandpa had prayed for my brother when he had cancer, often feeling ill himself as my brother went through his treatment. He told all of us grandchildren to mark 1 Thess. 4:11, which reads, "that you also aspire to lead a quiet life, to mind your own business, and to work with your own hands, as we commanded you," noting that that verse described our Grandpa. Grandpa was a craftsman; he made all kinds of beautiful and useful things out of wood. He was also an avid fisherman, and what a treat it was to go to Horseshoe Bend in the

Fever River and fish with him.

I must add, though, that, as sad as I was at Grandma's passing, the joy of the Lord did not leave me. He comforted me through all of my affliction and sorrow during that difficult year. Since Grandma and Grandpa Perkins were His, since they trusted in Him alone for their salvation, I knew I would see them again, just as I knew I would see my Dad again. It was a bittersweet kind of sorrow.

In my sorrow, God was speaking to me and comforting me. He speaks to His people. I know that God speaks to us, because the Bible says so, and because I've experienced hearing Him through scripture, His written word, in my heart and through other believers. For example, He spoke to me when I needed to know if my husband to be was the right one. He spoke to me when my dad was dying and gave me great assurance when I desperately needed it. He spoke to me in the midst of my cancer battle, and I clung to His words as a drowning woman clings to a life preserver.

3 GOD SEES AND HEARS

Dan and I were on our way home from an appointment with Dr. Lyss at Ste. Genevieve early in my cancer journey, when I read about Hagar in *The Peace and Power of Knowing God's Name* by Kay Arthur. (Arthur, Chapter 3) I mentioned earlier that, when we discovered I had breast cancer, we were in the midst of a serious conflict in our church. Dan realized we needed to be in a healthy church in order for me to get well, so he resigned from the pastorate. It was so hard. When Dan resigned, most of the congregation left the church. Thankfully, most of them are now in healthy churches. However, at the time, we felt that we had failed, and because a few families had wanted us to leave, we also felt rejected. In the midst of all this, I read the account of Hagar in Kay Arthur's book. The scripture passage is Genesis 16.

16 *Now Sarai, Abram's wife, had borne him no children. And she had an Egyptian maidservant whose name was Hagar.² So Sarai said to Abram, "See now, the LORD has restrained me from bearing children. Please, go in to my maid; perhaps I shall obtain children by her." And Abram heeded the voice of Sarai. ³ Then Sarai, Abram's wife, took Hagar her maid, the Egyptian, and gave her to her husband Abram to be his wife, after Abram had dwelt ten years in the* land of Canaan. *⁴ So he went in to Hagar, and she conceived. And when she saw that she had conceived, her mistress became despised in her eyes. ⁵ Then Sarai said to Abram, "My wrong be upon you! I gave my maid into your embrace; and when she saw that she had conceived, I became despised in her eyes. The LORD judge between you and me." ⁶ So Abram said to Sarai, "Indeed your maid is in your hand; do to her as you please." And when Sarai dealt harshly with her, she fled from her presence. ⁷ Now the Angel of the LORD found her by a spring of water in the wilderness, by the spring on the way to Shur. ⁸ And He said, "Hagar, Sarai's maid, where have you come from, and where are you going?" She said, "I am fleeing from the presence of my mistress Sarai." ⁹ The Angel of the LORD said to her, "Return to your mistress, and submit yourself under her hand." ¹⁰ Then the Angel of the LORD said to her, "I will multiply your descendants exceedingly, so that they shall not be counted for multitude."¹¹ And the Angel of the LORD said to her:*

> *"Behold, you are with child,*
> *And you shall bear a son.*
> *You shall call his name Ishmael,*
> *Because the LORD has heard your affliction.*
> *¹² He shall be a wild man;*
> *His hand shall be against every man,*
> *And every man's hand against him.*
> *And he shall dwell in the presence*
> *of all his brethren."*

¹³ Then she called the name of the LORD who spoke to her, You-Are-the-God-Who-Sees; for she said, "Have I also here seen Him who sees me?" ¹⁴ Therefore the well was called Beer Lahai Roi; observe, it is between Kadesh and Bered. ¹⁵ So Hagar bore Abram a son; and Abram named his son, whom Hagar bore Ishmael. ¹⁶ Abram was eighty-six years old when Hagar bore Ishmael to Abram. (Genesis 16, NKJV)

Kay's words are much better than mine are, and I recommend

you read her book. However, here is my interpretation of this scripture passage. Hagar was a maidservant, not very significant in the eyes of the world. Given to Abram as wife because of Sarai's impatience and unbelief. Not a marriage of love. But ...God gave her a baby. Now, she felt she had something to be proud of. Maybe a little too proud, at least from Sarai's point of view. And so her mistress was harsh with her. Hagar was rejected and outcast and it wasn't entirely her fault. After all, didn't Sarai want a baby?! Wasn't that the whole point? I don't blame Hagar for running away. Alone in the wilderness, discouraged. What was she to do? But the angel of the Lord visited her and gave her a promise. Her response? God sees me. In verse 13, "Then she called the name of the Lord who spoke to her, You-Are-the-God-Who-Sees for she said, "Have I also here seen Him who sees me?" God knows my situation. What comfort! The God who made all things sees not only nations and kings, but He sees me. He made me! He knows me! And He cares. Not only that, but He allows me to see Him! What did the Lord say to Hagar? "You shall call his name Ishmael [literally God hears] Because the Lord has heard your affliction." (Genesis 16:11) God not only sees us. He also hears us.

The implications for us are enormous. Whatever trial we're in, whatever situation we face, God sees it, He hears our prayers, and He allows us to see Him.

"O Lord, You have searched me and known me. You know my sitting down and my rising up; You understand my thought afar off. You comprehend my path and my lying down, And are acquainted with all my ways. For there is not a word on my tongue, But behold, O Lord, You know it altogether. You have hedged me behind and before, And laid Your hand upon me. Such knowledge is too wonderful for me; It is high, I cannot attain it. Where can I go from Your Spirit? Or where can I flee from Your presence? If I ascend into heaven, You are there; If I make my bed in hell, behold, You are there. If I take the

wings of the morning And dwell in the uttermost parts of the sea, Even there Your hand shall lead me And Your right hand shall hold me. If I say, 'Surely the darkness shall fall on me.' Even the night shall be light about me; Indeed the darkness shall not hide from You. But the night shines as the day; The darkness and the light are both alike to You. For you formed my inward parts; You covered me in my mother's womb. I will praise You, for I am fearfully and wonderfully made. Marvelous are Your works, And that my soul knows very well. My frame was not hidden from You, When I was made in secret, And skillfully wrought in the lowest parts of the earth, Your eyes saw my substance, being yet unformed, And in Your book they all were written, The days fashioned for me, When as yet there were none of them. How precious also are Your thoughts to me, O God! How great is the sum of them! If I should count them, they would be more in number than the sand; When I awake, I am still with You. (Psalm 139:1-18, NKJV).

I realized that the Lord knew exactly what was happening to us. He knew I would have cancer and was allowing me to walk through it. He knew we would feel rejected by some at our church. He was not at all surprised by what happened to us. He is sovereign, and He was allowing it all for a good purpose. Not only that, but He was walking through it with us. Honestly, we didn't always *feel* like He was there, but He was there, nonetheless. My friend, Jo Wallace, describes it. She said that she believes that, when His children are hurting, the Lord picks us up and holds us close. Yes, circumstances are hard and we suffer, but the Lord is right there, encouraging us, comforting us, urging us to persevere, just as He did for Hagar.

The Lord encouraged us in amazing ways that year. People we knew and people we didn't know gave us money to help us. A lady named Joyce brought us groceries many times and, along with the groceries, she would bring her famous freshly baked mincemeat cookies for us. What a treat! We all really enjoyed those cookies. I recall a man at church coming up to me one day and saying, "The

Lord told me to give you this," as he handed me a check. The Lord *saw*. He knew exactly what was going on with us.

In *The Red Sea Rules: The Same God Who Led You In Will Lead You Out,*, Robert Morgan writes, "Our whole perspective changes when, finding ourselves in a hard place, we realize the Lord has either placed us there or allowed us to be there, perhaps for reasons presently known only to Himself." (Morgan, p. 7) God sees the big picture. And – here's the key – from His perspective, the situation is well in hand – even when we feel like the world is spinning out of control.

In *Leadership That Works*, Leith Anderson describes a television program in which two World War II veterans recount the battle on D-Day at Omaha Beach.

> *The first interview was with a marine who landed on Omaha Beach. He recalled horrors that sounded like scenes from Steven Spielberg's Academy Award-winning movie, "Saving Private Ryan." The aging veteran recalled looking around at the bloody casualties and concluding, "We're going to lose!"*
>
> *The next interview was with a U.S. Army Air Corps reconnaissance pilot who flew over the whole battle area. He viewed the carnage on the beaches and saw the sacrifices on the hills, but he also witnessed the successes of the marines, the penetration by the paratroopers, and the effectiveness of the aerial bombardment. He looked at everything that was happening and concluded, "We're going to win!" Same battle, different perspectives. (Anderson, pp. 164-165, used with permission)*

Perspective – something God gave me over and over as I battled cancer. When we look from His perspective, we see that, indeed, Christ has already won the victory for those who put their trust in Him.

Have you trusted in Him? Have you given Him your self, your

life, your all? When we give ourselves to Him, He shows us that He has already given Himself for us. It's not an even exchange. He's God and we're His creatures, made in His image but marred by sin, yet He, as God the Son, willingly "emptied Himself, taking the form of a bondservant, and being made in the likeness of men," He became one of us and died for us to save us from sin and death. (Phil. 2:8, NKJV) Jesus, God in the flesh, rose again from the dead and He lives. He has won the victory from sin and death for us, so we can live in freedom from sin and victorious over death. If you've believed God for the first time, you may wish to pray. Here is a suggestion about what to pray:

> Lord God, I have not always believed you as I should, but I long to do so. I acknowledge that Jesus the Messiah is God in the flesh. He lived a perfect sinless life. He died to save me from my sins, which surely were deserving of separation from You. He rose from the dead and lives forever and is victorious. Please forgive me for my sins. Thank You for forgiving me. Thank you for giving me Yourself. I give You myself. Please do with me whatever You will. Help me to be obedient to you. Make me hungry to know You better and to study Your Word. Help me to believe You. In Jesus' name. Amen

If you have just prayed this for the first time, please tell someone; in particular, tell someone who can encourage you in your new adventure with the Lord. Find a church and find a Bible Study. Keep growing. The Lord will be faithful to complete the work He started. As the Apostle Paul wrote in Philippians, "He who has begun a good work in you will be faithful to complete it until the day of Jesus Christ." (Phil. 1:6, NKJV)

I agree with Beth Moore's message in her book, *Believing God*, when I tell you that I believe with all my heart, than what God wants from us, perhaps more than anything else is that we believe Him, that we trust Him, that we take Him at His word. For example, Hebrews 11:6 says, "Without faith it is impossible to please God, because anyone who comes to him must believe that He exists and that He rewards those who earnestly seek Him." What is the foundation of your relationship with your husband, your children, your friends? Is it not trust? Without trust, there can be no real intimacy. Without trust, where is love? I believe God longs for us to trust Him. Isaiah 43:10 tells us,. "You are my witnesses", declares the LORD, "and my servant whom I have chosen, so that you may know and believe me." God, the One who made Heaven and Earth, wants to have an intimate relationship with us. The God who spoke to little Hagar, will also speak to us, if we will listen. He will show Himself to us, if we will see. He will do things in and through us that we can't even imagine if we will believe Him.

My friend, Jean Seres, took me to her cabin in the country one day in July. We had a wonderful day, singing hymns and praises, praying, and talking about the Lord's great goodness! The cabin was decorated so sweetly and the atmosphere was so peaceful and quiet, I felt renewed. We enjoyed the singing of the birds and saw three redbirds, which Jean says are symbolic of hope from the Lord. Jean also gave me a praise acrostic, which I think she adapted from one by Jack Hayford. (Sutera, pp. 349-350)

Present your body a living sacrifice.
Raise your hands in praise.
Audibly compliment the Lord.
Invite the Holy Spirit to fill you with the fruit of the Spirit.
Sing a song of hope or deliverance.
Enter the day with faith.

I was trying to eat a healthy diet in order to help my body fight the cancer, taking care to eat more vegetables and use healthier fats. I was also thinking at that time about healthy nuts to eat and noted in my journal that almonds are particularly good for us. When the Lord instructed Moses about the lampstand for the Tabernacle, you probably remember that he said to decorate it with almond blossoms. In Jeremiah 1:11, when the Lords showed Jeremiah the branch of the almond tree, He said He was ready to perform His word. The significance of the almond tree is that it was known as the "waker" in Hebrew thought. Of all the trees in Israel, it "blossoms earliest, watching diligently for the opportunity to bloom." (*Spirit-Filled Life Bible*, p. 1056) God is the omniscient Sovereign of the universe. He is watching over us and He loves us. We ought to be awake, like the almond tree, watching for opportunities to believe God and step out in obedience to our Lord.

4 GOD ANSWERS AND HEALS

When I would go to Houston during the summer and early autumn of 2004 to have my chemotherapy and see Dr. Booser, I would stay with my cousins, Terry and Amy. They were incredibly kind and hospitable to me, and I enjoyed getting to know them better. I also enjoyed the patients and nurses I was able to meet at MD Anderson. One nurse said she had been reflecting on Psalm 37:4, "Delight yourself in the Lord, and He shall give you the desires of your heart." She said she had been praying about it, asking the Lord to give her more understanding of His word. I mentioned that my understanding of the verse is that God puts the desires in our hearts that He wants us to have. She said she hadn't thought of it that way, but she could certainly see how God had been changing the desires of her heart since she was saved. For example, she said she had a great desire to study His Word and talk about Him now. She was genuinely enthusiastic about His Word.

I met with Joy's Bible study in the Radiation Oncology Business Office. They were studying the *Forty Days of Purpose*. Joy was the lady who had helped Dan and me on our first visit to MD Anderson. I tried to visit her Bible study group every time I visited MD Anderson after that. It was precious to see the folks gathered to study God's Word and to pray for patients and one another. It was so fun to meet fellow believers and encourage one another! I also really enjoyed meeting and sharing with other patients at each visit. I asked the Lord to show me who to approach, how to encourage them and how to pray for them. That was a joy!

By September, my weight had dropped from about 130 lbs down to about 110 lbs, and the raw sensation in my gut and the feeling of starvation were taking their toll; thus, I was not always in a good mood. I found once again that the Lord's grace is sufficient. Thankfully, He would allow me to realize I was being irritable and repent, and He would again fill me with His joy and peace. My wonderful husband took the brunt of my bad moods, but he was always patient with me. He would cook for me, and one of the foods I liked best was potato-cauliflower soup. It was creamy and warm, and felt so good in my mouth that I cried tears of joy when I ate it. I had a Korean pumpkin soup recipe and that was also delicious, as were miso soup, chicken and rice soup, and just about any other soup we could think to make. It was all I wanted much of the time.

My brother was an encouragement to me as I walked through cancer treatment, since he'd also walked that path. Diagnosed with Ewing Sarcoma when he was eleven, my brother had done cancer back when treatment was much harder than it is now. He had been an example to me and to others at that time, because of his good attitude. Knowing that God had brought my brother through cancer was another thing that encouraged me in my own journey.

I have to pause and tell a story. My brother, of course, lost his hair due to the chemotherapy, and it was hard for him, because other kids can be mean. However, he found ways to joke about it. He used to tip his wig, as if it were a hat, startling everyone around him. Speaking of wigs, my son, Jacob, who was 2 years old, didn't like seeing me without hair. When I took off my wig at home, Jacob would get upset and would say, "Put your hair back on, Mommy."

My brother, partly because of his own experience with cancer, knew what to say and I was very grateful for that. One of the things he shared with me was something his pastor, John Heever, had shared with him: a passage from Exodus 15.

> ^{22}So Moses brought Israel from the Red Sea; then they went out into the Wilderness of Shur. And they went three days in the wilderness and found no water. ^{23}Now when they came to Marah they could not drink the waters of Marah, for they were bitter. Therefore the name of it was called Marah. ^{24}And the people complained against Moses, saying, 'What shall we drink?' ^{25}So he cried out to the Lord, and the Lord showed him a tree. When he cast it into the waters, the waters were made sweet. There He made a statute and an ordinance for them, and there He tested them, ^{26}and said, 'If you diligently heed the voice of the Lord your God and do what is right in His sight, give ear to His commandments and keep all His statutes, I will put none of the diseases on you which I have brought on the Egyptians. For I am the Lord who heals you." (Exodus 15:22-26, NKJV)

This was the first time in scripture that the Lord was called Jehovah Raphe, the Lord our Healer. According to John Heever, the wood that healed the water is a type of the cross. Kay Arthur also describes this idea in *The Peace and Power of Knowing God's Name*, as she refers to a desperate time in her life, when she said she didn't care what He did to her, if He'd just give her peace! And there beside her bed, she said she found that there is a Great Physician, who "applied the Cross to the bitter waters of her life, and [she] was healed of sin's mortal wounds." (Arthur, p. 75)

As I was studying my Bible, I was struck with the theme of water throughout the scriptures. Specifically, I noticed that Moses' name means "drawn out" and was given to him because Pharaoh's daughter drew him out of the water (Exodus 2:10). Later, when Moses arrived in Midian, he sat by a well and the daughters of Jethro, the priest of Midian, were there. When some shepherds tried to drive them away from the well, Moses helped them and watered their flock for them.

Of course, he ended up marrying one of Jethro's daughters.

My Bible study times had become so much more precious to me than they had ever been before. In Isaiah, one day I was struck by 57:17, "For the iniquity of his covetousness I was angry and struck him; I hid and was angry, and he went on backsliding in the way of his heart." My first thought was that that didn't apply to me. However, the Lord showed me otherwise. I had been for many years preoccupied with trying to figure out how to get out of debt, make better investments, and save more. I tried to figure out how to get more money to meet all these goals, and that was covetousness, since I was not content with what I had. I realized that, amazingly, for the first time in my adult life, I was not worrying about money like I had been, except for the day before, when I had been back to thinking about it; thus, reading Isaiah 57:17 served as a wake-up call for me

The passage continues in verse 18, "I have seen his ways, and will heal him. I will also lead him and restore comforts to him and to his mourners." I remembered that my husband had pointed out Isaiah 58:11 earlier in the year, which says, "The Lord will guide you continually, and satisfy your soul in drought and strengthen your bones. You shall be like a watered garden and like a spring of water, whose waters do not fail." You see, the water is God's provision of refreshment, strength, and life for His people. He delivered Israel using Moses, who was drawn out of the water. He provided for Jethro's daughters by having Moses draw the water for their flock.

I cannot help but weep, when I read what God said about Israel's idolatry in Jeremiah. "I remember you, The kindness of your youth, The love of your betrothal, When you went after Me in the wilderness…" (Jer. 2:2, NKJV) Later in the same chapter, God said, "For My people have committed two evils: They have forsaken Me, the fountain of living waters, And hewn themselves cisterns, broken cisterns that can hold no water." (Jer. 2:13, NKJV) Again God describes Himself as the source of water, the source of life, the source of all. The terrible thing is that we do exactly what Israel did in our own lives. We seek our own way, rather than seeking God, the source of living water, and this passage from Jeremiah points out to us the tragedy of our rebellion.

Jesus offered living water to the Samaritan woman at the well, and in Isaiah 58, He tells us that He will provide water for his people to satisfy them in drought and strengthen their bones. There is something else we need to know about this living water, which Jesus explained in John 7:37-39.

> *37 On the last day, that great day of the feast, Jesus stood and cried out, saying, "If anyone thirsts, let him come to Me and drink. 38 He who believes in Me, as the Scripture has said, out of his heart will flow rivers of living water." 39 But this He spoke concerning the Spirit, whom those believing in Him would receive; for the Holy Spirit was not yet given, because Jesus was not yet glorified. (John 7:37-39, NKJV)*

The living water thus is the Holy Spirit, God Himself. He is the source of all things for us. He is the One we need, not material things, not self-help manuals, not any worldly thing. We need God-Father, Son and Holy Spirit and Him alone.

The Lord was teaching me more and more to give up worrying about finances. I was doing some consulting work for Lockheed Martin and, one Saturday at the end of July, I was tempted to push myself to work, work, work in order to make enough to get all the bills paid. By this time, my husband's severance pay from the church had ended, and he didn't yet have an offer from a prospective employer, although he was diligently seeking a new position. One day I prayed, "Lord, you are the one who provides. I don't need to be all worried like this. I need to trust in you and in your provision." Two days later the Lord provided over $1000 from different people. Again, I was convicted about worrying so much.

In verse 26, God links health and healing to obedience. We know that sickness and death entered the world as a result of original sin. Sickness and death are not, of course, always the result of personal sin, but they can be. Scripture says that God disciplines His children, whom He loves. Therefore, sometimes He uses suffering to discipline us, but sometimes God has other purposes. He also uses suffering to prune us so we can bear more fruit. Jesus said, "I am the true vine, and My Father is the vinedresser. Every branch in Me that does not bear fruit He takes away; and every branch that bears fruit He prunes, that it may bear more fruit." (John 15:1-2, NKJV) God often uses suffering for His glory. For example, when Jesus healed the blind man in John 9, He told His disciples that the man's blindness was for the purpose of showing God's works. Therefore, we can summarize by saying that God uses suffering for His glory and for our good. I'm thankful God used my illness to help me to get more serious about living for Him, and to give me an encouraging testimony to give others who are struggling with a problem or crisis. 1 Peter 4:1 says that whoever has suffered in the flesh has ceased from sin. I don't understand this completely, except to say that when we give our suffering to God as an offering, he gives us grace to suffer gracefully. He is teaching us to persevere, to stay close to Him; He is teaching us to bear fruit.

Our Lord, Jesus Christ, is our example, as He suffered in redeeming us. Thanks be to our God who sent His Son to "be sin for us." (1 Cor. 5:21, NKJV) Think about how He was suffering as He prayed in the garden at Gethsemane, asking His Father to take away the cup He was about to drink but surrendering to the Father's will. "And being in agony, He prayed more earnestly. Then His sweat became like great drops of blood falling down to the ground." (Luke 22:44, NKJV) He chose to suffer in accordance with His Father's will in order to save us from sin and death. Isn't it clear that suffering is valuable to God?

When I was going through cancer, I read this anonymous poem, as quoted by Robert Morgan in *The Red Sea Rules*, The poem is also available on the internet. I think it illustrates very well the value of suffering and how God uses it in our lives, and it meant a lot to me when I read it.

When God wants to drill a man,
And thrill a man,
And skill a man;
When God wants to mold a man
to play the noblest part;
When He yearns with all his heart
to create so great and bold a man
that all the world might be amazed;
Watch His methods,
Watch His ways.
How He ruthlessly perfects
whom He royally elects.
How He hammers him and hurts him,
and with mighty blows converts him,
Into trial shapes of clay
* that only God understands,*
while his tortured heart is crying
and he lifts beseeching hands.
How He bends but never breaks,
when His good He undertakes.
How He uses whom He chooses
and with every purpose fuses him,
With mighty acts induces him
to try His splendor out.
God knows what He's about.
-Anonymous (from The Truth Renaissance)

The Lord also uses suffering to teach us about real joy. 1 Peter 4:13 tells us we should rejoice insofar as we share Christ's sufferings. Since our Lord has suffered far more than we ever will, we can know that He understands. When He walks through it with us, He is able to give us a joy that is truly beyond our comprehension. It is a miraculous kind of joy. Real joy doesn't come from feeling good physically. It doesn't come from everything going right in our world. It doesn't come from success or money. It doesn't even come from having a happy family. Real joy comes only from the Lord. When we suffer, we learn to look to Him alone, and when we do that, He fills us with joy unspeakable. While we are being molded into what God wants to make of us, we are getting to see God's splendor and majesty in a new way, a way that brings joy.

God uses suffering, but He also calls Himself our Healer, and His word is true. That said, if we suffer and get sick and die, what does this mean? Philippians 3:20-21 says, "For our citizenship is in heaven, from which we also eagerly wait for the Savior, the Lord Jesus Christ, who will transform our lowly body that it may be conformed to His glorious body, according to the working by which He is able even to subdue all things to Himself." I am certainly looking forward to the transformation! 1 Cor. 15:42b-44 adds, "The body is sown in corruption, it is raised in incorruption. It is sown in dishonor, it is raised in glory. It is sown in weakness, it is raised in power."

My mom was once talking with some pastors at a Disciple Training Seminar. The subject was Prayer, and Mom said she had a problem with it. The pastors asked why, and Mom explained that we had prayed and prayed for my dad when he was ill, but our prayer wasn't answered. One of the pastors asked, "What did you want to have happen?" Mom answered, "For my husband to be healed." The pastor said, "Well, isn't he?"

You see, God always heals His children, but sometimes it's not until we go to be with Him. That, however, is the most perfect healing of all. God's Word gives us a wonderful promise!

Behold, I tell you a mystery; We shall not all sleep, but we shall all be changed-in a moment, in the twinkling of an eye, at the last trumpet.

For the trumpet will sound, and the dead will be raised incorruptible, and we shall be changed. For this corruptible must put on incorruption, and this mortal must put on immortality. So when this corruptible has put on incorruption, and this mortal has put on immortality, then shall be brought to pass the saying that is written: "Death is swallowed up in victory."

"O Death, where is your sting?
O Hades, where is your victory?"

*The sting of death is sin, and the strength of sin is the law. But thanks be to God, who gives us the victory through our Lord Jesus Christ. Therefore, my beloved brethren, be steadfast, immovable, always abounding in the work of the Lord, knowing that your labor is not in vain in the Lord (*1 Cor. 15:51-58, NKJV)

In other words, keep your eyes on eternity and stand, celebrating the victory!

God does miracles. Look at His word. Miracle after miracle. God delivered His people from Egypt, parting the Red Sea, bringing water from the rock, sending food from Heaven. Jesus healed the sick, the lame, the blind. He raised people from the dead. He delivered people from demons. The apostles likewise prayed and saw God work mighty miracles amongst His people. God is still doing miracles today. If you aren't certain about this, find some books about missionaries and read them. You might read about Amy Carmichael, Hudson Taylor, Adoniram Judson, George Müller, Gladys Aylward, Don Richardson, Elisabeth Elliot, David Sitton, Saji Lukos, and so many others, You will be encouraged as you see what the Lord has done and is doing among His people.

What should we do then? We should seek God first whenever we are struggling with anything. We ask for physical healing, we ask for forgiveness, we ask for God's peace. As we are told in James, "Is any one among you suffering? Let him pray. Is any cheerful? Let him sing praise. Is any among you sick? Let him call for the elders of the church, and let them pray over him, anointing him with oil in the name of the Lord; and the prayer of faith will save the sick man, and the Lord will raise him up; and if he has committed sins, he will be forgiven." (James 45:13-15, NKJV) We pray, we ask, and then we wait upon the Lord. He will answer as He wills. We must acknowledge that the Lord of all is our Lord, too. Then, if we will humbly accept His will, even if His answer isn't what we hope for, He can make our bitter water sweet. When He speaks to us, and gives us His answer, we can stand on His answer, believing Him.

Because of Christ's shed blood for us, when we acknowledge Him as Savior and Lord, God says we are forgiven. That means we are forgiven. God says that when we are baptized into the body of Christ, we are dead to sin and alive to God. That means we are dead to sin and alive to God. Because Jesus has won the victory over sin, we can walk in our daily lives in victory over sin. When He says you're healed, you are healed. When He says you're His child, you are His child. When He tells a woman He will be a husband to her who has no husband, He will. When He says that He is all we need, then He is. Beth Moore put it so well. "We are not God. Give up trying. And give up asking anyone else to try. Our part is to believe God. His part is to be God and to do what is ultimately and eternally best. He alone knows the ultimate objective to which He aligns every divine act on behalf of His children. All are dearly loved. All are intricately planned for. God never sits on His hands." (Moore, *Believing God, p. 245*) What confidence we can have, knowing that our God is utterly faithful, and that His word can be trusted. We can stand on it.

After about five months and eight chemo treatments, it was apparent to all of us that the Lord was healing me. Dr. Booser was obviously very pleased with my progress. When he told me I had almost complete remission, I really wasn't surprised! My thought was that I was glad that everyone was seeing what the Lord was doing in me!

Please read Isaiah 55, then consider prayers you have prayed and how God has answered. Try to see the good He has done through your suffering. If you can't see it now, rest assured that one day, you'll understand.

Jane Runkle

5 GOD PROVIDES

In October of 2004, we received the news that Dan had gotten the position he had applied for at Lockheed Martin in Fort Worth. The official package came on his birthday. What a birthday present that was! We thanked and praised the Lord once again! There were many answered prayers at this time. We praised the Lord that Grace's problem with crossing her eyes was not serious and we were so thankful that Sarah was accepted into the gifted program at her school. I was thankful for my friendship with our pastor's wife. Oh, there was a lot of answered prayer that October! Then in November, we found out that I had complete remission. Our joy was overflowing!

In November of 2004, we moved to Fort Worth, Texas. We were quite excited about it, and we were not disappointed. As we drove into Texas, we saw many cows and picturesque ranch scenery, including large gates emblazoned with brand designs. I've always liked cows. I guess it's because I associate them with visiting my grandparents in Wisconsin. At any rate, I was very happy to see them. I was joyful but I was also still quite weak and needed a lot of help, and it was amazing to see how the Lord gave me the help and encouragement I needed.

We stayed in an apartment while we were house hunting in Fort

Worth, and, when it was time to pack up the house in Cape Girardeau, my husband travelled there to supervise the move. In the course of conversation, he shared with the movers the events that had led up to that time and the way the Lord was helping us through it all. We finally moved into our new house two days before Christmas! When our movers unloaded the truck, they noticed the Christmas tree box, and they kindly decided to unpack the tree and set it up for us. We were really touched by the love they showed to our family!

Our parents once again came to our aid. This time, my mother-in-law was there to help me unpack boxes. I was very weak and had to rest frequently. She told me, "Just sit and tell me where you want things to go." I tended to get analysis paralysis, and she would say, "Let's just get things put away. You can always rearrange it later." I pass that advice on folks that are moving, as I found it very helpful.

My surgery, a modified radical mastectomy, was scheduled for January, and my mother flew down to Fort Worth, so she could take me to Houston and stay with me there, since I still needed further treatment at MD Anderson. Since Dan had just started a new job, he could not get away to be with me. In addition, he needed to be with the kids and help them adjust to their new surroundings. Thankfully, my mother-in-law and later my father-in-law were willing and able to stay in Fort Worth with Dan and the kids and helped them.

Dr. Ross did my surgery, and I have since heard that he is probably one of the most thorough breast cancer surgeons anywhere. I enjoyed chatting with the anesthesiologist I met with before my surgery, a professor of anesthesiology and cardiology with a degree in electrical engineering, and a PhD in toxicology, besides the MD, of course. We had quite an interesting conversation about measuring the speed of thought. After the surgery, Dr. Ross' assistant told me that they found no invasive cancer left in my breast; there was only DCIS. All but one of the nineteen the lymph nodes removed were clear, and the one that wasn't had only a very small spot left in it.

A Girl Scout troop provided mastectomy patients at MD Anderson with heart-shaped pillows to use after mastectomy surgery. I chose one that was white on one side and magenta on the other. I found that holding the pillow under my arm cushioned my sore chest, and the pillow was also useful for tucking between the seat belt and my chest when I was in the car. The pillow was so helpful that, a few years later, when my mother had breast cancer, I made one for her to use after her surgery. She, in turn, found the pillow so helpful that now she leads a group of women at her church in making mastectomy pillows to supply several hospitals in her area.

I wanted to have my radiation therapy in Fort Worth, so I wouldn't have to be away from home. However, that was not to be. My friend, Joy, the lady who worked in the radiation oncology business office at MD Anderson, told me, "I've chosen your radiation oncologist for you!" She arranged a meeting in the atrium at MD Anderson, and there I met Dr. Strom. I told him I really wanted to have my radiation therapy in Fort Worth, but he said I needed to have it there at MD Anderson. He told me that, at MD Anderson, they do radiation therapy differently than it is done anywhere else. He told me that my plan would be the most difficult he had done, but that he was the one to do it. The problem was going to be getting sufficient radiation to my sternum without damaging my heart. Another difficulty would be getting sufficient radiation to the left side of my thyroid gland without killing the gland. I agreed to return to MD Anderson for my radiation therapy and began it in February.

My mom lived in Houston with me, and my in-laws helped my husband with the kids at home in Fort Worth. It was a blessing getting to spend so much time with my mom. When I felt up to it, we toured the Houston area, enjoying museums, historical homes, and the bluebonnets in the hill country near Brenham. One home sticks in my memory, as it was the home of the Hogg family, including daughter Ima. She was a highly respected philanthropist and art collector.

We also enjoyed meeting other patients at MD Anderson. I was so impressed by the women who were there alone. There was one lady from Mexico, who was there for treatment by herself, and she went to evening concerts on her own. I recall that she invited us to go with her. I think my mom may have gone to one, but I was usually too tired in the evening to go anywhere. I don't know how she did it. There was also a sweet lady from Monroe, Louisiana, with whom we sometimes ate breakfast in the hotel lobby.

Mom and I also enjoyed visiting various Houston churches, including First Baptist, Beth Moore's home church. We visited her Sunday school class a couple of times, and it was great! On our second visit, we chatted with Beth Moore briefly after class, and she prayed for me. I had also gotten to meet Babbie Mason at Southcliff Baptist, our church in Fort Worth, and she also had prayed for me. It was fun getting to meet these well-know Christian women and finding out how very genuine they are. Overall, it was a difficult time, but Mom and I managed to have a lot of fun, too. By this time, I only had to have the Herceptin once every three weeks rather than every week, which freed up our schedule a bit and was a welcome relief.

Chemotherapy had been a big challenge, but I found the challenge wasn't over. Radiation therapy was difficult as well. Since my throat had to be irradiated because of the cancer found on my thyroid and in a lymph node in my neck, I once again had difficulty eating. About a third of the way through the treatment, swallowing became very painful. If I swallowed too much or swallowed incorrectly, I'd jump from the pain. Thankfully, the pain lessened after a few days, and, while it remained uncomfortable, I was able to eat. Although I was eating much more than I had on chemo, I was not able to gain weight. In addition, the skin on my chest burned and felt tight. Sometimes it would feel like the left side of my chest was clamping down. It still happens at times, but much less frequently than it did during therapy. I was very thankful for the help of my physical therapist, Ron. Because of his good work, I regained the full range of motion of my left arm. The Lord was using many people to help carry me through.

Dan and the kids visited about halfway through the radiation therapy. Jacob, who was 3 years old at this point, was happy my hair was growing back. He said that, without hair, I was "Jane", but, with hair, I was "Mommy." Sarah was eight-years-old at this point and Grace was five. Sarah and Grace would remember, of that time, that they knew I was sick, but had no idea how critically ill I was. In part, they didn't know because of their youth, but I believe it was also because of the joy the Lord gave me. Jacob, on the other hand, was too young to remember much about it at all.

When I saw Dr. Booser for an appointment one day during the radiation therapy, I asked his opinion about getting my right breast removed. Since he didn't think getting the right breast removed would affect my prognosis, I didn't consider it any further. I was still trying to decide about having reconstruction but finally decided against it. The risks inherent in reconstruction surgery are really much greater than with a mastectomy, and I just couldn't see taking on the risk for a merely cosmetic surgery. I was alive and cancer-free and was ready to be finished with all of the medical stuff! I must mention here how thankful I am for the skill, wisdom and knowledge the Lord gave Dr. Booser, Dr. Ross and Dr. Strom, my oncologists at MD Anderson. I firmly believe that they are the best in the world at their specialties.

When my radiation therapy was finished, I was allowed to ring the bell hanging in the hallway outside the rooms where the radiation therapy is administered. Ringing the bell is an MD Anderson tradition. I invited my therapists, some family and friends. I read Psalm 30, of course, as it was my theme Psalm for that period. The little ceremony was quite moving to me. I was quite certain then and still am that the Lord truly has healed me; He has turned my mourning to dancing.

Returning home required a major adjustment. I had work to do once again, and it took several weeks for me to get enough strength back to be of much use at home. I also had radiation pneumonitis, but, after a one-month course of prednisone, the cough was gone, and I felt much better.

I went back to MD Anderson in June for a CAT scan and ultrasound and everything looked good. Dr. Strom said that my sternum had an abnormal area on the CAT scan, likely due to scar tissue and recalcification, and he said it would probably never look normal. As long as there was no change to it, however, he said the physicians reviewing future scans would be able to see that no cancer was present. Dr. Strom was grinning from ear to ear when I saw him for that appointment, and I could tell Dr. Booser was very happy, too. I was well!!

Even more amazing than the miracle God did in healing me was the miracle He did in giving me joy and peace as I walked under the shadow of death. This is not to say that I didn't have any struggles in this regard, but, as I have described, the Lord was with me and He used my trial to draw me nearer to Him and to teach me to trust Him more.

I've mentioned that I had always struggled with worrying about finances. My husband had chided me about that, frequently reminding me that the Lord was our Provider. However, while I was going through cancer, it seemed that we had every reason to be worried about money. Medical bills were coming in, and some of them were large, since our deductible was so high. We still had to pay a mortgage. We still needed groceries, and, since we were trying to eat more healthy food, including organically grown fruits and vegetables, I was spending more on food than ever before. My husband had resigned from the church he had pastored. My consulting work was not bringing in much income, since the progress of the work had slowed due to my illness. One would think, given my history, I would have been very worried about our financial situation. However, the Lord brought me to the place where I wasn't worried at all. How could this be? The only way I know to explain it is that it was a miracle of the Lord. He had provided peace and joy for me. I just knew He would provide the rest. For the first time in my life, I really wasn't worried about finances. I knew that the Lord would provide, and He did. You see, the Lord is always our provider. We may think that we provide or that our employer provides, but that just isn't so. God is the One who provides for us!

God's provision was abundant. Our new church, Lynwood Baptist in Cape Girardeau, Missouri, had set up a fund for us. Our church family brought us groceries and gave us money. Friends and relatives from further away sent us support. Our children's preschool offered to take care of our kids at no charge as much as needed. Our physicians worked with us on the bills, as long as we paid something regularly. Old friends from college and seminary days sent us money and gifts to cheer us. The family of our sister-in-law, Melinda Runkle, also helped us, even though they did not know us very well. The outpouring of love for us was incredible. It was the Lord's provision. All outward appearances indicated we should have gone deeply into debt during those months. By the Lord's grace, we did not, and we are so thankful.

I want to be clear about something here. The Lord is faithful to provide what we need when we trust in Him. What we think we need and what He knows we need may be different. At times, God's people do suffer privation. At times, that is part of His will for us. Remember, in God's economy, suffering is valuable. What is it that we really need? We need Him. If privation will draw us nearer to Him, He will allow it. We hear too many people these days thinking that God has promised us material prosperity. That is simply not true. He has promised to provide for us what we need, but that may not include material things. We must learn to trust Him no matter what our circumstances, and, let's face it, circumstances can get quite awful.

I think often about our brethren around the world who are persecuted for the faith. When I think about them, I wonder how I would do in their shoes. I used to worry about whether I would stand firm in the faith if I were persecuted. What if my children were threatened? Would I stand for the Lord or would I weaken and fall? Would I forsake my Lord? The thought terrified me. What if I did? How would I stand? I now know that the Lord would give me the grace to stand. I believe that's how the martyrs stood throughout history. I believe that's how our brethren in the persecuted church around the world are able to stand. They stand by God's grace. He can miraculously enable us to walk through situations we could never endure on our own. Philippians 4:6-7, says, "Be anxious for nothing, but in everything by prayer and supplication with thanksgiving, let your requests be made known to God; and the peace of God, which surpasses all understanding, will guard your hearts and minds through Christ Jesus." (Phil. 4:6-7, NKJV)

Give your worries to the Lord. I know it is hard. We leave our burdens at His feet, only to pick them up again. In Philippians, the apostle Paul tells us, "I know how to be abased, and I know how to abound. Everywhere and in all things I have learned both to be full and to be hungry, both to abound and to suffer need. I can do all things through Christ who strengthens me." (Phil. 4:12-13, NKJV) How wonderful that we can rely on Christ's strength in every situation!

God wants us to be still, and know that He is God. (Psalm 46:10). We need to spend time with Him, praising Him and believing Him. Jesus said, "...do not worry about your life, what you will eat or what you will drink; nor about your body, what you will put on. Is not life more than food and the body more than clothing? Look at the birds of the air, for they neither sow nor reap, nor gather into barns; yet your heavenly Father feeds them. Are you not of more value than they?" (Matthew 6:25-26, NKJV) We need to trust Him, to depend on Him, to believe all He tells us in His Word, and to obey Him in everything.

In November of 2005, about six months after I finished treatment, I was at MD Anderson for my six-month checkup. During the ultrasound exam, the radiologist found something suspicious. I asked what it could be and the radiologist said it had to be a new metastasis. I told her I didn't know what it was, but I knew it wasn't cancer. When she left the room to try to call my oncologist, I asked the Lord what He was doing with me. He first gave me Psalm 15 to read, and I did and saw I needed to repent for a bad attitude toward someone, so I prayed about my bad attitude. You see how hardheaded I can be. The Lord sometimes has to use rather difficult circumstances to get my attention! Then I asked Him for another word. I wanted to stand and believe, but I needed some encouragement. He then gave me Psalm 33, and some words popped out at me. "The LORD brings the counsel of the nations to nothing; He makes the plans of the peoples of no effect. The counsel of the LORD stands forever, The plans of His heart to all generations." (Psalm 33:10-11, NKJV) I said, "Lord, you told me you were going to heal me, and You healed me. I'm going to stand on that, because Your word stands forever."

When the radiologist came back in, she said she had decided to do a biopsy. While I waited for the results, I continued to pray, and a word came to my mind. It was "cyst." Imagine my joy when the radiologist returned with the results saying, "It came back ganglion cyst." I told her that the Lord was showing us that He is utterly faithful. When God says He will do a thing, He surely does it.

Now, I'm not saying that God promises always to do what we ask. We ask for physical healing, certain material provisions, restoration of a relationship. He doesn't always give us what we think we need, but He always does what is best. What I am saying is that, when He speaks to us, we need to believe what He says and stand on it.

The Lord's provision builds our faith. When I received my cancer diagnosis, I thought back to the Lord's provision throughout my life, even from the very beginning of it. I mentioned earlier that my birth was difficult, but the Lord brought me through it. He provided for us to move to Palatine after my dad's passing, He gave us three children and we can attest to His miraculous provision in their births, He provided work for my husband, healing for me, and it goes on. I could share with you time after time when God provided for us. He is providing for you, too. You may want to take some time to jot down instances in which God has provided for you. You may use the chart in the study helps at the end of this book. Count your blessings and thank Him for His provision.

God provides His grace! We can do all things through Christ. (Phil. 4:13) When we abide in Him, when we spend time in His word, His word becomes alive and active in us. God's Word is different from any other book. Beth Moore makes the point that "God's words are omnipotent" and, because we've been created in His image, "our words are potent." (Moore, *Believing God, p.135*) Our words can be potent for good or for evil. God desires for us to believe the truth and to speak the truth. That is why we study scripture, learn scripture, pray scripture, and act on scripture. Unlike any other book, God's Word has the power to change us, and it is vitally important that we believe all of it, not just the bits that suit us. As the apostle Paul told Timothy, "All Scripture is given by inspiration of God, and is profitable for doctrine, for reproof, for correction, for instruction in righteousness, that the man of God may be complete, thoroughly equipped for every good work." (2 Tim 3:16-17, NKJV)

God's Word is Truth. God's Word is Power. God's Word is Wisdom. Let's all of us today commit to listening to God, studying His word, believing Him, trusting Him, and enjoying the peace and joy that only He can give. Praise Jesus! He has won the victory. Let's walk in it!!

I suggest you take some time to choose a Psalm (86, 91, 30, 23, and 27) to pray aloud, and then praise the Lord, using scripture to refer to God's attributes and praising Him from your heart.

6 CONCLUSION

It has now been more than ten years since my cancer journey began. The Lord continues to carry me faithfully through every trial and difficulty. I continue to receive Herceptin infusions every three weeks in order to prevent a recurrence of cancer. This, in itself, is a great blessing, since it allows me to sit in the chemo room at my oncologist's office and share what God has done with other cancer patients. It seems to be encouraging to them, which is why I wanted to share these lessons with you.

In addition, the Lord used the lessons I learned through cancer to change my heart about my priorities in life. I had been very career-oriented before cancer; however, during cancer, I realized that the greatest work God gave me to do was to raise my children to know Him. I've gotten to home school my children for the last eight years, and what a blessing that has been! I'm also learning more and more the blessing of becoming a submissive wife. My husband ever becomes dearer to me. He is such a servant-leader. I'm so grateful for his constant support and encouragement. I'm also so thankful for all the ways God changed me through cancer. As I said at the time, it was a hard year but it was a good year. It was definitely worth all the suffering.

Through cancer, I learned in a more powerful way than ever

before that God sees what we go through. He hears us when we pray. He speaks to us in many ways but primarily through His Word. He answers our prayers. Sometimes the answers are "yes" and sometimes they are "no." Sometimes He tells us to wait, but always His answers are best. God heals us; perhaps not always when and how we would like, but He is indeed our Healer. He is caring for His own. If you have trusted Jesus as your Lord and Savior, you are in His hands. Nothing can separate you from His love, and He will safely bring you home. If you have not trusted Jesus, please trust Him today. The Bible's promises are yours only if you trust and obey Him.

Your sufferings and your lessons are certainly not exactly the same as mine. However, I hope that this little book has encouraged you to trust the Lord through it all. In Him is peace. In Him is life. In Him is victory! The Lord Jesus Christ has overcome sin and death for you. Walk in the victory. "Weeping may endure for a night, But joy comes in the morning." (Psalm 30:5b, NKJV)

STUDY HELPS

This book is adapted from a retreat given for some ladies from my mother's church. I included study questions and suggestions for meditation in the ladies' retreat packets. I want to share those with you also, as you may wish to do some further study on your own. The Study Helps begin on the next page.

Study of 2 Chronicles 20
Scripture Passage: 2 Chronicles 20:1-30

What was the problem King Jehoshaphat faced (v. 1)?

What did he do (v. 4)?

On whom did he rely (v. 12)?

Did the Lord answer (v. 15)?

Whose battle was it (v. 15)?

In whom did King Jehoshaphat say to believe (v. 20)?

Whom did Jehoshaphat say to believe (v. 20)?

What is the difference between the two? Do you think this is significant?

Why should Israel (and why should we) believe the prophets?

About what did the prophets speak (see Jeremiah 1:4-10)?

How did the people respond (v. 21)?

What is significant to you about their response?

What did the Lord do next (v. 22-24)?

Jane Runkle

Trusting the Lord with Your Problems

Think about problems you've faced and complete the following table:

Problem	I relied on:	Results

In the results section, don't just write whether the problem resolved as you originally wanted it to, but write how you felt. Were you frantic or were you at peace? If the problem was not resolved as you originally wanted it to, can you see good that the Lord brought out of it?

70

Answered Prayer

Use the table below or your own notepaper to jot down some prayers you have prayed and how God answered. Write down your thoughts about God's answer from a heavenly perspective.

Prayer	How God Answered	My Thoughts

Additional Questions for Meditation and Study

How has God revealed Himself to you through His word?

Name some scriptures that have meant a lot to you.

How is seeing things from God's perspective comforting?   Can you give examples from your own life?

How is seeing things from God's perspective challenging? Can you give examples from your own life?

What are your greatest challenges right now? For what are you hoping in these circumstances? Does God will seem clear or not?

Describe a time when you stepped out in faith and obedience to God.

Read Matthew 9:20-22. What does the Lord say about your faith in this passage? What is your response?

Read Matthew 9:27-30. What does the Lord say about your faith in this passage? What is your response?

Read Hebrews 11:6. What does the Lord say about your faith in this passage? What is your response?

Read Matthew 17:14-21. What does the Lord say about your faith in this passage? What is your response?

Read Ephesians 1:18-21. Focus on verse 19a. What does the Lord say about your faith in this passage? What is your response?

What is the fruit of worrying? In contrast, what is the fruit of trusting the Lord? You may want to share examples from your own life.

Read 1 John 5:14-15. Discuss what those verses mean to you.

Read 1 Cor. 10:1. How does this encourage you to look at the health laws God gave to Israel? If you are interested, you may wish to read the book by Rex Russell listed in the bibliography.

BIBLIOGRAPHY AND RECOMMENDED READING

Anderson, Leith, *Leadership That Works*, Bloomington, MN, Bethany House Publishers, 2001.

Arthur, Kay, *The Peace and Power of Knowing God's Name*, Colorado Springs, Waterbrook Press, 2002.

Blackaby, Henry and Richard Blackaby, *Experiencing God*, Nashville, Lifeway, 1990.

"Breast Cancer Treatment," Web. http://www.mdanderson.org/patient-and-cancer-information/cancer-information/cancer-types/breast-cancer/treatment/ index.html, July 18, 2015.

Christensen, Evelyn, *What Happens When God Answers Prayer*, Colorado Springs, Victor Books, 1994.

Dravecky, Dave and Jan, *The Encourager*, Vol. 12, No. 1. Web. http://www.endurance.org/wp-content/uploads/2011/01/SeeingClearly_Vol.12No.1_WinterSpring2006.pdf.

Fintel, William A. and Gerald R. McDermott, *Cancer: A Medical and Spiritual Guide for Patients and Their Families*, Grand Rapids, BakerBooks, 2004.

Gilham, Annabell, *The Confident Woman: Knowing Who You Are in Christ*, Eugene, Oregon, Harvest House Publishers, 1993.

Hurd, Stephen, "God Has Not Given Us the Spirit of Fear," Integrity, 2001.

The Spirit-Filled Life Bible, Ed. Jack Hayford, Nashville, Thomas Nelson Publishers, 1991.

McWherter, Joseph, Avoiding Breast Cancer While Balancing Your Hormones Dallas, A. E.Rosebud, 2005.

Moore, Beth, *Believing God,* Nashville, Broadman and Holman, 2004

Moore, Beth, *Voices of the Faithful,* Brentwood, Tennessee, Integrity Publishers, 2005.

Morgan, Robert J., *The Red Sea Rules: The Same God Who Led You In Will Lead You Out,* Nashville, Thomas Nelson, 2001.

Rothschild, Jennifer, *Walking by Faith: Lessons Learned in the Dark,* Nashville, Genevox Music 2003.

Russell, Rex, *What the Bible Says about Healthy Living: Three Biblical Principles That Will Change Your   Diet and Improve Your Health,* Ventura, California, Regal Books, 1996.

Sutera, Henrietta, *How to Live the Wonderful Christian Life*, Maitland, FL, Xulon Press, 2009.

"When God Wants to Drill a Man," Web. http://thetruthrenaissance.wordpress.com/2010/09/14/poetry-when-god-wants-to-drill-a-man, July 15, 2014.

ABOUT THE AUTHOR

Jane Runkle has previously published technical works, but this is her first foray into non-technical writing. She holds a doctorate in Engineering Science from Louisiana State University and worked as an engineer for about sixteen years altogether. She has three children and has been homeschooling for eight years. In addition, she currently teaches high school math and science courses for homeschooled students in Fort Worth, TX.